DANCE

Breakdancing

by Wendy Garofoli

Consultants:
Rokafella and Kwikstep
hip-hop instructors and founders of Full Circle Soul Dance Company

Capstone
press

Mankato, Minnesota

Snap Books are published by Capstone Press,
151 Good Counsel Drive, P.O. Box 669, Mankato, Minnesota 56002.
www.capstonepress.com

Library of Congress Cataloging-in-Publication Data

Garofoli, Wendy
    Breakdancing / Wendy Garofoli
    p. cm.—(Snap books. Dance)
    Summary: "Describes breakdancing, including history, training, moves,
and competition"—Provided by publisher.
    Includes bibliographical references and index.
    ISBN-13: 978-1-4296-0122-1 (hardcover)
    ISBN-10: 1-4296-0122-1 (hardcover)
    1. Breakdancing—Juvenile literature. I. Title.
GV1796.B74G37 2008
793.3—dc22
                                          2006102786

Editor: Becky Viaene

Designer: Veronica Bianchini

Photo Researcher: Wanda Winch

Photo Credits:
Capstone Press/Karon Dubke, all except pages 5, 26–27, 29, 30, and 32; Capstone Press Archives, 30; Corbis/Danser/
Nicolas Six, 29; Courtesy of the author Wendy Garofoli, 32; Getty Images Inc./Reportage, 26–27; The Image Works/
SV-Bilderdienst/K Brenniger, 5

Acknowledgements:
Capstone Press would like to thank dance instructors Amy Sackett, Damian Day "Daylight" and Jason Noer, the
students of Collective, and Dance Endeavors Studio, in Bloomington, Minnesota.

1 2 3 4 5 6 12 11 10 09 08 07

Table of Contents

Chapter One

BREAKDANCING

Make Some Noise

A DANCER QUICKLY SPINS ON THE GROUND FROM ONE SMOOTH MOVE TO THE NEXT. THE CROWD AROUND THIS B-GIRL GOES CRAZY WHEN SHE BUSTS OUT HER FINAL POSE.

For years, people have been amazed by this style of dance called breaking, b-boying, or b-girling. You also may have heard it called breakdancing. But most hip-hop dancers call it breaking.

If you want to be the one in the middle getting down, you first have to get up on your breaking history. Breaking is one of the four parts of hip-hop, which also includes DJing, MCing, and graffiti. Hip-hop's rich culture began in the Bronx, New York, in the early 1970s.

Breaking Through The Years

By the early 1980s, breaking's popularity was soaring. It was in music videos, TV shows, and movies. B-boys were making noise, and Hollywood took notice.

In the 1980s, guys weren't the only ones busting moves. Women came forward to showcase their skills too. In Europe, Baby Love, Bubbles, and Karima showed that women have what it takes to break. In the United States, Honey Rockwell, Rokafella, Asia-One, and other b-girls held their own with the b-boys. Go girls!

As breaking's popularity grew, people started to feel that the dance was "played out." The late 1980s were a rough time for breaking. Hip-hop MCs and DJs who once supported breaking now turned away from it. But some b-boys and b-girls continued breaking in theater productions and on New York City streets. Media coverage helped breaking's popularity explode again in the mid-1990s.

Today, you can see breaking in movies such as *You Got Served, Brown Sugar,* and *Honey.* B-boy and b-girl performance groups bring their skills to the stage. And there are conventions and festivals dedicated to breaking held across the globe!

Chapter Two

Before You Break

WHETHER YOU'RE DANCING WITH A TIGHT-KNIT GROUP, CALLED A CREW, OR DANCING SOLO, BREAKING IS YOUR CHANCE TO SHOW YOUR STYLE.

Besides your moves, one of the best ways to be original is by the clothing you wear. Stay simple but stylish with tracksuits, sneakers, wristbands, and hats. Loose-fitting tracksuits let you move and keep you comfy. Your shoes should have good grip and be lightweight. Use your wristbands to wipe sweat off of your forehead. You and your crew can also wear bold colors or matching jerseys to stand out from the crowd.

BREAKDANCING

The main important thing about breaking and winning is being original. Really, it's about how original you are and how confidently you rock your style.

–Big Tara
New York City b-girl

9

Shape Up

Before you jump right in, you should prepare your body for breaking by stretching and building strength. Stretch by rolling out your wrists, shoulders, and neck. It's a good idea to stretch your lower body too. Bend down and touch your toes, or sit in a straddle position.

Breaking puts a lot of stress on the upper body, so you should do exercises like pull-ups and push-ups to gear up your arms. Sit-ups will help strengthen your abdominal muscles.

Breaking has served as a life lesson. I dealt with a lot of hard times and persevered. I slayed a lot of demons with this dance.

-Rokafella
hip-hop instructor and co-founder of Full Circle Soul Dance Company

Chapter Three

BREAKDANCING

Gettin' Down

When a breaker does her moves, a circle of people called a cypher forms around her. People watch and clap while they wait to move to the middle of the circle. Start by just watching to get a feel for what breaking looks like. You can also watch a breaking video or Internet clips. Then try a breaking class or learn moves from a friend.

Beginning breaking can be rough on your body. Expect to have some bruises and blisters during the first few weeks of practice. But bruises and blisters are nothing to be embarrassed about. They're just proof that you're gettin' down!

A Solid Start

Before you begin a set of breaking moves, you'll need to impress the crowd. Toprocking is a solid way to start.

But this style is more than just an attention-grabber. Toprocking is also your time to feel the beat of the music.

Toprocking is danced on top, meaning you stay standing up. The rocking part comes from the way your body rocks back and forth when you dance.

Kick Step Out

A main toprock move is a kick step out. This name isn't formal, but breakers will know the move as soon as they see it.

Start by kicking out with your right foot. Put your foot down and step your left foot to your left side. Bring your feet together. Now switch legs and try kicking with your left foot. You can also step back or forward by kicking one leg and stepping behind or in front with the other foot.

This move will feel choppy at first. Smooth it out by adding a little hop to your step. Adding arm movements will give your moves style and flow.

6-Step

When you think about breaking, you probably imagine dancers on the ground with their feet flying fast around them. This style is called floor work or downrock. The most important move to learn is the 6-step. In a 6-step, your feet should travel around your body in a circle.

Step one: Start in a push-up position with your knees slightly bent. Lift your left hand and place your right leg straight out where your left hand was.

Step two: Next, tuck your left leg under your behind.

Step three: Place your right leg bent underneath you so you are in a squat.

Step four: Shift weight onto your left arm and cross your left leg in front of your right leg.

Step five: Step straight back with your right foot.

Step six: Step your left foot back to get to step one.

Start Spinning

Add excitement to your set of moves by adding spins. Spins will have your body moving like a merry-go-round in no time.

You'd probably love to start with headspins, but spinning takes practice. Start simple with one of the easiest spins—the buttspin. Sit on the ground with your legs pointed toward the ceiling. Kick your right leg over your left leg.

Want something more difficult? Try the handglide, or handspin. Kneel on the floor and place your right elbow into your stomach. Place your right hand flat on the ground. Lift up your legs and use your left arm to spin your body. See how long you can spin!

Freezes

Throw up a peace sign or wrap your arms across your chest and hold that position. You just did a very basic freeze. Freezes are used to add pauses for effect or to finish a routine.

A good freeze to try is the rollback freeze. Lay on your back with your knees pulled toward your chest. Put your hands on your hips and kick your legs in the air. Then position your legs however you like, hold still, and you'll have a fantastic freeze.

Once you have the rollback freeze down, try the chair freeze. Start by lying on your right side. Bend your right arm up under your body.

Now, bend your right leg up and cross your left leg over it. Finish this move by bending your left arm and placing it above your head.

Advanced Moves

You may have seen breakers do amazing things for commercials on TV. Once you've mastered the basic moves try some advanced moves, like a one-handed spinning handstand, called the 1990. Time to take your b-girling to the next level!

To do a 1990, start by standing. Place your legs a few feet apart and put your arms at your sides. Twist your body to the right. Bend down and place your right hand in front of your right foot. Then put your left hand down and kick your left leg up. Next, raise your right leg up. Your legs will make a "V" shape in the air. Then raise your left arm and twist to the left. What a way to impress a crowd!

Butterfield School Library
1441 W. Lake Street
Libertyville, Illinois

25

Chapter Four

Show Me What You Got

A BIG PART OF B-BOY AND B-GIRL CULTURE IS BATTLING.

BREAKDANCING

In a battle, crews and individual dancers challenge other dancers' skills. If one person does really well, another will step forward and try to outdo her. The person with the loudest crowd response wins. Most battles are unplanned events that happen in the streets or in clubs. But formal, organized battles also take place each year.

BREAKDANCING

Battle of the Year

At organized competitions, crews battle for respect and prize money. One of the largest breaking contests is the Battle of the Year (BOTY), which is held once each year in Germany. B-boys and b-girls from across the globe come to compete. Crews of eight people or fewer have only six minutes to impress the judges. Judges look for creativity, difficulty of moves, and how well the crew performs together. Only the best of the best make it here.

But remember that being the best breaker doesn't mean you have to do the hardest steps. If you have confidence, style and originality, you'll win the respect of other breakers. As you practice, you'll learn, when you can, change a move to make it yours.

Even after you've conquered the advanced levels, you'll find there will always be something else to learn, so keep practicing!

Glossary

crew (KROO)—a group of dancers who practice and perform together

cypher (SY-fuhr)—a circle that forms around a breaker to give space to dance

DJ (DEE-jay)—a person who spins records for a dance party or hip-hop performance

freeze (FREEZ)—a dramatic pause in a breaking routine

graffiti (gruh-FEE-tee)—pictures drawn or words written with spray paint on buildings, bridges, and trains; most graffiti is illegal.

MC (em-SEE)—a person who rhymes to the DJ's mix

media (MEE-dee-uh)—TV, radio, newspapers, and other communication forms that send out messages to large groups of people

Fast Facts

Early breakers were influenced by many things, including gymnastics and martial arts.

When breaking first began, some gangs used it as a nonviolent way to settle disagreements.

In the 1980s, the United States Postal Service released a hip-hop culture stamp.

Read More

Craig–Quijada, Balinda. *Dance for Fun!* Activities for Fun! Minneapolis: Compass Point Books, 2004.

Hatch, Thomas. *A History of Hip-Hop: The Roots of Rap.* High Five Reading. Bloomington, Minn.: Red Brick Learning, 2006.

Kramer, Nika. *We B*Girlz.* New York: PowerHouse Books, 2005.

Internet Sites

FactHound offers a safe, fun way to find Internet sites related to this book. All of the sites on FactHound have been researched by our staff.

Here's how:

1. Visit *www.facthound.com*

2. Choose your grade level.

3. Type in this book ID **1429601221** for age-appropriate sites. You may also browse subjects by clicking on letters, or by clicking on pictures and words.

4. Click on the **Fetch It** button.

Facthound will fetch the best sites for you!

About the Author

Wendy Garofoli is a writer for several different magazines, including *Dance Spirit*, *Dance Teacher*, *Pointe*, and *Cheer Biz News*. Before becoming a full-time writer, she co-directed a jazz and hip-hop company named Impulse and performed with Decadancetheatre, an all-girl hip-hop dance group.

INDEX